LIVING THE GOD LIFE

JOHN ORTBERG

TO:

FROM:

May God shower you with the blessings of the truly good life.

Living the God Life: Finding God's Extraordinary Love in Your Ordinary Life
Copyright © 2004 by John Ortberg
ISBN 0-310-80195-8

Requests for information should be addressed to:
Inspirio, the gift group of Zondervan
Grand Rapids, Michigan 49530
http://www.inspiriogifts.com

Compiler: Doris Rikkers
Editor: Tom Dean
Design Manager: Val Buick
Design: Kirk DouPonce, UDG|Designworks

Printed in China
04 05 06/HK/ 4 3 2 1

JOHN ORTBERG

Finding God's Extraordinary Love in Your Ordinary Life

LIVING THE GOD LIFE

inspirio

The gift group of Zondervan

We *love* because he FIRST loved US.

1 JOHN 4.19

Love
Is
All
AROUND

Living in God's love requires new eyes. We must learn to continually see God's grace at work all around us. It was Ian Pitt-Watson, a beloved teacher, who suggested that we are all God's much-loved rag dolls.

love \luv\ *n.* a warm personal attachment or deep affection for another person

unconditional love \un' ken dish' e nl luv\ *n.* to love no matter what

grace \gras\ *n.* God doing in and for us what we cannot do ourselves

The Much-Loved
Rag Doll

Her name was Pandy. She had lost a good deal of her hair, one of her arms was missing, and, generally speaking, she'd had the stuffing knocked out of her. She was my sister Barbie's favorite doll.

She hadn't always looked like this. She had been a personally selected Christmas gift by a cherished aunt who had traveled to a great department store in faraway Chicago to find her. When Pandy was young and a looker, Barbie loved her. She loved her with a love that was too strong for Pandy's own good. When Barbie went to bed at night, Pandy lay next to her. When Barbie had lunch, Pandy ate beside her at the table. When Barbie could get away with it, Pandy took a bath with her. Barbie's love for that doll was pretty nearly a fatal attraction.

By the time I knew Pandy, she was not a particularly attractive doll. In fact, she was a mess. But my sister Barbie loved that little rag doll still. She loved her as strongly in the days of Pandy's raggedness as she ever had in her days of great beauty.

Other dolls came and went. Pandy was family. Love Barbie, love her rag doll. It was a package deal.

Once we took a vacation from our home in Rockford, Illinois, to Canada. We had returned almost all the way home when we realized that Pandy had not come back with us. No other option was thinkable. My father turned the car around and we drove back to Canada.

The years passed, and my sister grew up. She outgrew Pandy. By now the only logical thing left to do was to toss her out. But this my mother could not do. She wrapped Pandy with exquisite care in some tissue, placed her in a box, and stored her in the attic.

More years passed. My sister got married and moved far away. She had three children, the last of whom was a little girl named Courtney, who soon reached the age where she wanted a doll. No other option was thinkable. Barbie went back to Rockford, back to the attic, and dragged out the box. By this time, though, Pandy was more rag than doll. My sister took her to a doll hospital and Pandy became once again as beautiful on the outside as she had always been in the eyes of the one who loved her.

When Pandy was young, Barbie loved her. She celebrated her beauty. When Pandy was old and ragged, Barbie loved her still. Now she did not simply love Pandy *because* Pandy was beautiful, she loved her with a kind of love that *made* Pandy beautiful.

More years passed. My sister's nest will soon be emptied. Courtney is a teenager now. And Pandy? Pandy's getting ready for another box.

For God so loved the world that he gave his
only Son, so that everyone who believes in him
may not perish but may have eternal life.

JOHN 3.16

For while we were still weak, at the right time Christ
died for the ungodly. But God proves his love for us
in that while we still were sinners Christ died for us.

ROMANS 5.6,8

In this is love, not that we loved God
but that he loved us and sent his Son
to be the atoning sacrifice for our sins.

1 JOHN 4.10

CREATED IN LOVE

We are God's rag dolls. He knows all about our raggedness, and he loves us anyhow. Our raggedness is no longer the most important thing about us. Raggedness is not your destiny, nor is it mine. We may be unlovely, yet we are not unloved.

There is a love that creates value in what is loved. There is a love that turns rag dolls into priceless treasures. There is a love that fastens itself onto ragged little creatures, for reasons that no one could ever quite figure out, and makes them precious and valued beyond calculation. This is a love beyond reason. This is the love of God. This is the love with which God loves you and me.

Love is why God created us in the first place. Theologians speak of the fact that God created everything freely, not out of necessity. This is a very important idea—it means that God did not make us because he was bored, lonely, or had run out of things to do. God did not create us out of need. He created us out of his love.

God, who needs nothing, loves into existence wholly superfluous creatures in order that He may love and perfect them.

C. S. Lewis

So Much Love

G od filled the world with beauty and mystery, with waterfalls and sunsets and glaciers and tropics and banana cream pie, but God said, "I don't just love you this much."

God gave you a mind, the ability to know right from wrong, to choose good life, but God said, "I don't just love you this much."

God gave you people. Teachers, friends, heroes, persons with whom to know the joy of intimacy and community. But God said, "I don't just love you this much."

Then God gave Jesus. Jesus was God's ultimate attempt to let us know what we mean to him. He was led to the cross to pay the debt we couldn't. He was led to the cross and God said, "Now you can be freed from every regret. No more guilt. Every demand of justice satisfied. Now at last you understand the place you have in my heart."

He was led to the cross and Jesus said, "I love you this much."

How great is the love the Father has lavished on us,
that we should be called children of God!
And that is what we are!

1 JOHN 3.1 NIV

For I am convinced that neither death, nor life,
nor angels, nor rulers, nor things present, nor things
to come, nor powers, nor height, nor depth, nor
anything else in all creation, will be able to separate us
from the love of God in Christ Jesus our Lord.

ROMANS 8.38-39

We have known and believe
the love that God has for us.

1 JOHN 4.16

YOU ARE GOD'S BELOVED

There is in every human heart an inextinguishable desire to be someone's prince, someone's princess. We want to be beloved.

The Bible says we are. The writers of Scripture use the most extravagant images available to convince us of this. God's love for us is the love of a friend who would sacrifice his life for the one he loves, the love of a father for a runaway son, the love of a mother that will not allow her to forget her child. God's love for us is more passionate than the heart of the most passionate groom for his bride.

You ARE the beloved of God.

This cry of our heart to be loved is only the faint echo of God's desire to love us. Before you were ever born, you were beloved in the mind of God. This is the deepest secret to your identity. It cannot be earned or won, only gratefully embraced.

This is the ineffable and infinite mercy of God which the slender capacity of man's heart cannot comprehend and much less utter—the unfathomable depth and burning zeal of God's love toward us.

MARTIN LUTHER

A Father's Unconditional Love

T hen Jesus said, "There was a man who had two sons. The younger of them said to his father, 'Father, give me the share of the property that will belong to me.' So he divided his property between them. A few days later the younger son gathered all he had and traveled to a distant country, and there he squandered his property in dissolute living. When he had spent everything, a severe famine took place throughout that country, and he began to be in need. So he went and hired himself out to one of the citizens of that country, who sent him to his fields to feed the pigs. He would gladly have filled himself with the pods that the pigs were eating; and no one gave him anything. But when he came to himself he said, 'How many of my father's hired hands have bread enough and to spare, but here I am dying of hunger! I will get up and go to my father, and I will say to him: "Father, I have sinned against heaven and before you; I am no longer worthy to be called your son; treat me like one of your hired hands."' So he set off and went to his father.

"But while he was still far off, his father saw him and was filled with compassion; he ran and put his arms around him and kissed him. Then the son said to him, 'Father, I have sinned against heaven and before you; I am no longer worthy to be called your son.' But the father said to his slaves, 'Quickly, bring out a robe—the best one—and put it on him; put a ring on his finger and sandals on his feet. And get the fatted calf and kill it and let us eat and celebrate; for this son of mine was dead and is alive again; he was lost and is found!' And they began to celebrate."

LUKE 15:11-24

You live in the hand of God. God's heart is filled with tenderness and delight at the mere thought of you. When you love somebody and you think about them, it makes you smile. That's how it is for God when he thinks about you.

You ARE the beloved of God.

NOTHING you will ever do could make God love you more than he does right now: not greater achievement, not greater beauty, not wider recognition, not even greater levels of spirituality and obedience.

NOTHING you have ever done could make God love you any less: not any sin, not any failure, not any guilt, not any regret.

The irony is we spend our lives trying to earn the love that we can only receive when we *admit* our poverty of spirit.

To learn to live in the love of God is the challenge of a lifetime.

A Party of Grace & Love

This story by Tony Campolo took place while he was traveling in Hawaii.

At three in the morning, I wandered into a diner. The only other customers were a group of prostitutes who had finished for the night, one of whom (Agnes) mentioned that tomorrow was her birthday, and that she had never in her life had a birthday party.

After they left, I found out from Harry, the guy behind the counter, that they came each night to this diner. I asked if I could come back the next night and throw a party. Harry said okay.

At 2:30 the next morning, I was back. I had made a sign that read, "Happy Birthday, Agnes!" By 3:15 every prostitute in Honolulu was in the place. It was wall-to-wall prostitutes . . . and me!

At 3:30, the door of the diner swung open, in came Agnes, and we all screamed "Happy Birthday!" Never have I seen a person so flabbergasted. When we finished singing, her eyes moistened; when the cake was carried out, she started to cry.

Harry gruffly mumbled, "Cut the cake, Agnes. We all want some cake."

"Look, Harry, is it OK if I keep the cake a little while?"

"Sure. Take the cake home if you want."

She carried that cake out the door like it was the Holy Grail. We stood there motionless, a stunned silence in the place. Not knowing what else to do, I broke the silence by saying, "What do you say we pray?"

Looking back on it now, it seems more than strange for a sociologist to be leading a prayer meeting with a bunch of prostitutes in a diner in Honolulu at 3:30 in the morning. But then it just felt like the right thing to do. I prayed for Agnes: for her salvation, that her life would be changed. That God would be good to her.

When I finished, Harry said; "Hey, you never told me you were a preacher. What kind of church do you belong to?"

I answered, "I belong to a church that throws birthday parties for prostitutes at 3:30 in the morning."

Harry waited a moment, and answered, "No, you don't. There's no church like that. If there was, I'd join it."

Wouldn't we all? Wouldn't we all love to join a church like that? That's the kind of church Jesus came to create. I don't know where we got the other one that's so prim and proper. But anyone who reads the New Testament knows Jesus loved to lavish grace on the left-out and the used-up and the put-down. The sinners loved him because he partied with them.

That story illustrates the church the way it's supposed to be. A group of rag dolls who have received love even though they know they didn't deserve it, who then extend it to others because they refuse to allow raggedness to keep them from loving. Because love is God's signature. And grace makes love strong.

Grace is the one thing the church has to offer that cannot be obtained anywhere else.

For by grace you have been saved through faith, and this is not your own doing; it is the gift of God.

EPHESIANS 2.8

But God, who is rich in mercy, out of the great love with which he loved us even when we were dead through our trespasses, made us alive together with Christ—by grace you have been saved.

EPHESIANS 2.4-5

Since all have sinned and fall short of the glory of God; they are now justified by his grace as a gift, through the redemption that is in Christ Jesus.

ROMANS 3.23-24

The Wonder of Grace

A s a Christian I must remember not only that I was saved by grace, but that I am loved *this day* by grace. God did not save me by grace only to decide that now he will base how he feels about me on my spiritual performance yesterday. God's love is *always* a gracious love.

God himself says you are chosen. You are wanted. God desires you for his family. Today. This is the wonder of grace.

By grace we have been made alive. Now you are alive to God. You have strength to endure, power to serve, a reason to hope. Death itself has no hold over you. This is the wonder of grace.

By grace we are forgiven. God took our indebtedness and guilt and nailed it to the cross. He erased the bill, destroyed the IOU, and set you free. Unburdened. Cleansed. You can live with a heart as light as a feather. Today—no matter what you did yesterday. This is the wonder of grace.

Therefore, we can live in joy. We can have unshakable confidence—today, tomorrow, the next day, and every day through eternity. We can offer love to every human being, however ragged. This is the wonder of grace.

N O W we have received from God nothing but love and favor, for Christ has pledged and given us his righteousness and everything he has; he has poured out upon us A L L his treasures, which no man can measure and no angel can understand or fathom, for God is a glowing furnace of love, reaching even from the earth to the heavens.

MARTIN LUTHER

THE GIFT OF LOVE

To be loved means to be chosen. The sense of being chosen is one of the very best gifts love bestows on the beloved. Someone has seen me as a unique person, and that someone desires to come closer to me, to be on the same side as I'm on. Someone believes I have a significant contribution to make.

Love confers a kind of chosenness on the one who is loved. Love whispers, I choose you. I want to be on your side. And for ragged people, for people with misshapen spirits and crooked hearts and lopsided souls, this is life.

When I am chosen, I am seen as unique. **Objects may be indistinguishable from each other. But each human being cries out to be noticed as special, as not just one more of the same.**

When I am chosen, I am recognized as someone who has something to contribute. **My uniqueness is positive. I have a gift that will make a difference. I have something that will help the team. Chosen people are significant. Their biographies get written and read because their stories matter.**

When I am chosen, it means somebody wants me. **I am not isolated, unconnected. I am desired. I belong.**

When God chooses us, he imparts all the good implied by the choosing. In our fallen world, however, the term CHOSEN has a fourth implication that is not present in the heart of God. To be chosen in our world almost always means to be chosen at the expense of someone else.

God does not choose in that way, though. In God's love, my chosenness never comes at anyone else's expense. God chooses, or loves, each of his children with infinite uniqueness. His plan is for my chosenness to enhance the lives of others, not diminish them. In God's plan, those who are chosen are always chosen to serve.

"To be loved uniquely—for one's special self—is to be loved as much as we need to be loved." This is what God does; he loves each of us uniquely.

God chose us in Christ before the foundation of the world to be holy and blameless before him in love. He destined us for adoption as his children through Jesus Christ, according to the good pleasure of his will, to the praise of his glorious grace that he freely bestowed on us in the Beloved.

EPHESIANS 1.4-6

Jesus said, "If you belonged to the world, the world would love you as its own. Because you do not belong to the world, but I have chosen you out of the world—therefore the world hates you."

JOHN 15.19

But you are a chosen race, a royal priesthood, a holy nation, God's own people, in order that you may proclaim the mighty acts of him who called you out of darkness into his marvelous light.

1 PETER 2.9

Safe in God's Love

Some time ago I wanted to tell my three children how they could live in the loving care of God, so I told them the story of a movie called *The Bear*. It is the saga of a tiny bear cub whose mother dies. The cub survives, but the viewer knows that his long-term chances are nil. Then the unexpected happens. The little cub gets adopted by an enormous kodiak. This giant is always watching over the cub. He protects it. He teaches the cub how to be a bear. Everything the father bear does, the cub imitates. You watch this and are filled with hope—the cub has a future. He's going to live.

One day they get separated. The little bear can't see his father anywhere. The mountain lion sees his opportunity. He comes swiftly, silently, face-to-face with the cub; he is about to spring. The little bear rears up on his hind legs, lifts his paws, and tries to growl fiercely, but the best he can manage is a frightened squeak. The mountain lion is not convinced. Both the cub and his attacker know he is about to die.

The camera focuses on the mountain lion, whose face suddenly registers a look of fear. He stops snarling, turns, and slinks away.

The camera pans back, and we see what we did not know was there; we see what the little bear cannot. Behind that little bear is the great kodiak, standing on his hind legs, his massive body poised to save his son with a single swipe.

Big paws. Fierce growl.

Then we know. The little bear had nothing to worry about. The cub couldn't see him or hear him, but the father was there all the time. That forest was a perfectly safe place for the little cub to be. The father could be trusted, even when he seemed to be absent.

This story is true for you and me as well. You will take risks in life, and you will face problems. This is part of life and growth, and I would not spare you from it if I could. But I do want to spare you from one thing. Sometimes when you are afraid, you may be tempted to think you're all alone. You may think no one sees or cares, that you are on your own.

When that happens, I want you to remember the bear. Remember that Someone is watching over you. You may not be able to see or hear him. But you are never out of his sight. You are never out of his care.

The LORD will not let your foot be moved;
he who keeps you will not slumber.
He who keeps Israel
will neither slumber nor sleep.

The LORD is your keeper;
the LORD is your shade at your right hand.
The sun shall not strike you by day,
nor the moon by night.

The LORD will keep you from all evil;
he will keep your life.
The LORD will keep
your going out and your coming in
from this time on and forevermore.

PSALM 121:3-8

Living in God's Peace

A mother wakes up during a thunderstorm. She hurries to her son's room after a particularly bright flash of lightning, knowing he will be terrified. To her surprise, he is standing at a window.

"I was looking outside," he says, "and you'll never guess what happened, God took my picture."

He was convinced God was at work and therefore that the universe was a perfectly safe place for him to be.

Being convinced that we are safe in God's hands is what Paul called "the peace of Christ."

Ask yourself this question: What would my life look like if I lived in the settled conviction that, because of God's character and competence, this world is a perfectly safe place for me to be?

My anxiety level would go down. I would have the settled trust that my life is perfectly at rest in the hands of God. I would not be tormented by my own inadequacy.

I would be an unhurried person. I might be busy, I might have many things to do, but I would have an inner calmness and poise that comes from being in the presence of God. I would not say so many of the foolish things I now say because I speak without thinking.

I would not be defeated by guilt. I would live in the confidence that comes from the assurance of God's love.

I would trust God enough to risk obeying him. I wouldn't have to hoard. Worry makes me focus on myself. It robs me of joy, energy, and compassion.

A person in whom the peace of Christ reigns would be an oasis of sanity in a world of pandemonium.

A community in which the peace of Christ reigns would change the world.

With this magnificent God

positioned among us, Jesus brings us

the *assurance* that our universe

is a perfectly SAFE place to be.

DALLAS WILLARD

For the mountains may depart
and the hills be removed,
but my steadfast love shall not depart from you,
and my covenant of peace shall not be removed,
says the LORD, who has compassion on you.

ISAIAH 54.10

Where can I go from your spirit?
Or where can I flee from your presence?
If I ascend to heaven, you are there;
if I make my bed in Sheol, you are there.
If I take the wings of the morning,
and settle at the farthest limits of the sea,
even there your hand shall lead me,
and your right hand shall hold me fast.

PSALM 139.7-10

Be strong and courageous;
do not be frightened or dismayed,
for the LORD your God is with you
wherever you go.

JOSHUA 1.9

Finding Contentment

Ethicist Richard Mouw was asked by some minister friends to attend a Rolling Stones concert at the Rose Bowl because, they said, they wanted to do some theological reflection on popular culture. So there they were, a group of middle-aged clerics on the Voodoo Lounge tour, calling their teenage children and holding out their cell phones so their kids would hear the Red Hot Chili Peppers warming up the crowd and believe their fathers were really there.

One of the ministers asked Mouw, "There are 85,000 people here; more than will be in all the churches and synagogues of Pasadena this weekend. What would you say to them if you had the chance?"

Mouw had no idea—until Mick Jagger started singing the Stones' signature song, "Satisfaction." Eighty-five thousand people started chanting along: "I can't get no satisfaction. (But I try. . .)"

Mick Jagger and 85,000 fans had come to the same conclusion as the writer of Ecclesiastes. Great food, great sex, boundless fame, endless wealth, enormous power—these we might be clever enough to attain, but not satisfaction. All these pursuits turn out to be trivial pursuits. A hunger keeps resurfacing that they cannot satisfy.

Why is it that we are so frustrated, so discontent? The amazing answer, in part at least, is that our frustration comes from God himself. God knew that after the Fall we would try to set up other gods, try to give our lives to the pursuit of pleasure or wealth or power or status. So he said that one of the results of the Fall would be that none of these things would be able to bring us "soul satisfaction." Our pursuit of them will always involve a measure of discontent, of disappointment.

God's hope is that we will stop searching for infinite satisfaction from finite objects. His hope is that the day will dawn when we realize we "can't get no satisfaction," however hard we try, and come home. Frustration in this sense is a kind of gift. It is one of the forms God's love takes for people who might otherwise throw their lives away on trivial pursuits.

Pursue above all the kingdom of God and his righteousness, Jesus said, and everything else will be thrown in in the bargain. Apart from this, everything else is a trivial pursuit.

The human heart has been dissatisfied since we left Eden. But God loves us even with our ragged, insatiable desires. In fact, contentment can only be found in authentic living that is grounded in his love. As Augustine said, "You have made us for yourself; and our hearts are restless till they find their rest in Thee."

Living in God's
love and care
is the *only*
HOPE
for *satisfaction* of
the human heart.

Ho, everyone who thirsts,

come to the waters;

and you that have no money,

come, buy and eat!

Come, buy wine and milk

without money and without price.

Why do you spend your money

for that which is not bread,

and your labor for that which does not satisfy?

Listen carefully to me, and eat what is good,

and delight yourselves in rich food.

Incline your ear, and come to me;

listen, so that you may live.

I will make with you an everlasting covenant,

my steadfast, sure love for David.

ISAIAH 55.1-3

THE SECRET TO A
JOY-FILLED LIFE

God holds out joy for each of us. We are all made to do and see things in a unique way—God has designed you to know the joy of being a teacher or helper or encourager or designer—and when you find it and offer it up you will know joy. And God has made you to know the joy of receiving and celebrating the gifts of those around you. If you offer your gifts (let go of them) and humbly receive the gifts of others, your joy will be made complete.

If you don't, if you go through life wishing for joy that belongs to others, if you live a life of comparison or competition, you will end up with no joy at all.

I have found that there is a tremendous joy
in giving. It is a very important part of the joy
of living.

WILLIAM BLACK

Real joy comes not from ease or riches or
from the praise of men, but from doing something worthwhile.

SIR WILFRED GRENFELL

If you want to do the work of God, pay attention to people. Notice them. Especially notice the people nobody else notices. When you pay attention to someone, when you focus totally on them, you say, "You are the most important thing in my world right now."

Love is a form of work. Scott Peck writes, "The principal form that the work of love takes is attention. When we love another person we give him or her our attention; we attend to that person's growth."

God pays close attention to us: "Even the hairs of your head are numbered," Jesus said. We often take it as a sign of love if someone is able to notice a haircut or a change in hairstyle. God has numbered our every hair. If one falls out, he notices. (He may not replace it, unfortunately, but he notices!) God notices things your mother has never even thought about. And when we live in the love of God, we begin to pay attention to people the way God pays attention to us.

Jesus said, "Are not two sparrows sold for a penny?
Yet not one of them will fall to the ground
apart from your Father. And even the hairs
of your head are all counted. So do not be afraid;
you are of more value than many sparrows."

MATTHEW 10.29-31

A Love Story

One of the Pharisees asked Jesus to eat with him, and he went into the Pharisee's house and took his place at the table. And a woman in the city, who was a sinner, having learned that he was eating in the Pharisee's house, brought an alabaster jar of ointment. She stood behind him at his feet, weeping, and began to bathe his feet with her tears and to dry them with her hair. Then she continued kissing his feet and anointing them with the ointment. Now when the Pharisee who had invited him saw it, he said to himself, "If this man were a prophet, he would have known who and what kind of woman this is who is touching him—that she is a sinner." Jesus spoke up and said to him, "Simon, I have something to say to you." "Teacher," he replied. "Speak." "A certain creditor had two debtors; one owed five hundred denarii, and the other fifty. When they could not pay, he canceled the debts for both of them. Now which of them will love him more?" Simon answered, "I suppose the one for whom he canceled the greater debt." And Jesus said to him, "You have judged rightly."

Then turning toward the woman, he said to Simon, "Do you see this woman? I entered your house; you gave me no water for my feet, but she has bathed my feet with her tears and dried them with her hair. You gave me no kiss, but from the time I came in she has not stopped kissing my feet. You did not anoint my head with oil, but she has anointed my feet with ointment. Therefore, I tell you, her sins, which were many, have been forgiven; hence she has shown great love. But the one to whom little is forgiven, loves little."

Then he said to her, "Your sins are forgiven. Your faith has saved you; go in peace."

LUKE 7.36-50

Love is never so fully love as when it gives.

In addition to attending to God, I am called to attend to the people who mean so much to him. The work of love is the work of paying attention. Love notices. LOVE LISTENS. Love remembers.

This is your day. This is your opportunity to do the work of God. Don't miss it. If you do, you don't get it back. Night is coming. *Don't miss the day.*

For we are what he has made us,
created in Christ Jesus for good works,
which God prepared beforehand
to be our way of life.

Ephesians 2.10

Therefore be imitators of God,
as beloved children, and live in love,
as Christ loved us and gave
himself up for us, a fragrant offering
and sacrifice to God.

Ephesians 5.1-2

As God's chosen ones,
holy and beloved,
clothe yourselves with compassion,
kindness, humility, meekness, and patience.
Bear with one another and,
if anyone has a complaint against another,
forgive each other; just as the Lord
has forgiven you. . . . Above all,
clothe yourselves with love,
which binds everything together
in perfect harmony.

COLOSSIANS 3.12-14

We are above all things loved—

that is the GOOD NEWS of

the gospel. . . . To come together

as people who believe that just

maybe this gospel is actually

true should be to come together

like people who have just won

the Irish sweepstakes.

The miracle of God's love for ragged people is that in a whole universe that obeyed his will, in a cosmos of beauty and order, his concern should extend to one crooked little planet in one insignificant corner of one small galaxy in the whole of his work. It would be easier for him just to erase it. One rebel planet seems too small to be worth his time to run after, seems like a trivial pursuit.

The miracle of God's love is that he should become a human being and work as a carpenter and grow hungry and tired and weak and should teach and even cry for you and me. For in the end, the story of God's love for this world is the story of a pursuit that is trivial no longer. Not after God became man. Not after the cross.

Beloved, since God loved us so much,
we also ought to love one another.
No one has ever seen God; if we love one another,
God lives in us, and his love is perfected in us.

1 JOHN 4.11-12

I pray that, according to the riches of his glory, he may
grant that you may be strengthened in your inner being
with power through his Spirit, and that Christ may
dwell in your hearts through faith, as you are being
rooted and grounded in love. I pray that you may have
the power to comprehend, with all the saints, what is
the breadth and length and height and depth, and to
know the love of Christ that surpasses knowledge,
so that you may be filled with all the fullness of God.

EPHESIANS 3.16-19

We know love by this, that he laid down his life
for us—and we ought to lay down our lives
for one another. Little children, let us love, not in
word or speech, but in truth and action.

1 JOHN 3.16,18

God lets rain fall on both the thankful and the unthankful. He gives money, property, and all types of things from the earth to the very worst scoundrels. Why does he do this? He does it out of GENUINE, pure love. His heart is full and overflowing with love. He pours his love over everyone, leaving no one out, whether good or bad, worthy or unworthy. This love is righteous, godly, whole, and complete. It doesn't single out certain people or separate people into groups. He freely gives his love to all.

MARTIN LUTHER

God's love has

no limits,

his grace has

no measure,

his power has

no boundaries

known unto men.

God Speaks to His People

One of the most beautiful passages in Scripture is found in Isaiah 43. God is speaking to his people, and although the words are addressed to Israel, they are yours and mine as well. Read them, and allow them to be God's word to you.

I have summoned you by name; you are mine.
When you pass through the waters,
    I will be with you;
and when you pass through the rivers,
    they will not sweep over you.
When you walk through the fire,
    you will not be burned;
    the flames will not set you ablaze.
[God is a great big God,
though you can't see him or hear him,
he is always with you.
He never takes his eyes off you.]
For I am the Lord, your God,
    the Holy One of Israel, your Savior. . . .
Since you are precious and honored in my sight,
    and because I love you.

ISAIAH 43.1-4 NIV

Perhaps you could write down that last phrase on a card and carry it with you: "You are precious and honored in my sight, and I love you." You are the beloved of God. What more do you need to achieve or prove or acquire? You are the beloved of God. Who else do you need to impress? What other ladder do you need to climb?

You are the beloved of God. What are you going to add to your resume that is going to top that?

What if you were to make your life an experiment of living in the love of God? Every morning, when you wake up, let your first words be, "I am the beloved." Each night, when you go to sleep, let your last words echo, "I am the beloved."

Write those words down, and carry them with you. When you're tempted to despair because you've blown it, take out the card and look at it. When you wake up and you're tempted to be overwhelmed by all you have to do, take it out and look at it.

Take it out when you are tempted to sin, to dishonor God, when you are tempted to lash out in anger and hurt someone, or deceive someone, or use someone; when you're afraid; when you're anxious; when you're alone. Remember and feast on the words that give life: "I am the beloved. I am loved by God."

The God who loves you is greater than you can imagine. You may not be able to see him or hear him, but he is here. He is watching.

The *joy*

of the LORD

is your

strength

NEHEMIAH 8:10

Turning
HO-HUM
INTO
Dee-Dah

dee dah \de' daa\ *adj.* denoting joy

dee dah day dance *n.* (1997) a relatively simple dance expressing great joy

joy \joi\ *n.* a feeling or state of extreme delight or happiness

The Dance of Joy

Some time ago I was giving a bath to our three children. I had a custom of bathing them together, more to save time than anything else. Johnny was still in the tub, Laura was out and safely in her pajamas, and I was trying to get Mallory dried off. Mallory was out of the water, but was doing what has come to be known in our family as the Dee Dah Day dance. This consists of her running around and round in circles, singing over and over again, "Dee dah day, dee dah day." It is a relatively simple dance expressing great joy. When she is too happy to hold it in any longer, when words are inadequate to give voice to her euphoria, she has to dance to release her joy. So she does the Dee Dah Day.

On this particular occasion, I was irritated. "Mallory, hurry!" I prodded. So she did—she began running in circles faster and faster and chanting "dee dah day" more rapidly. "No, Mallory, that's not what I mean! Stop with the dee dah day stuff, and get over here so I can dry you off. Hurry!"

Then she asked a profound question: "Why?"

I had no answer. I had nowhere to go, nothing to do, no meetings to attend, no sermons to write. I was just so used to hurrying, so preoccupied with my own little agenda, so trapped in this rut of moving from one task to another, that here was life, here was joy, here was an invitation to the dance right in front of me—and I was missing it.

So I got up, and Mallory and I did the Dee Dah Day dance together.

Unlike mine, Mallory's life is unstuffed. She just lives. While she's taking a bath, it's a dee dah day moment. And when it is time to get dried, that's another one. After she's dry, it will be time for another. Life is a series of dee dah day moments. Each moment is pregnant with possibility. Mallory doesn't miss many of them. She is teaching me about joy.

JOY is at the heart of God's plan for human beings. Joy is at the heart of God himself. We will never understand the significance of joy in human life until we understand its importance to God. I suspect that most of us seriously underestimate God's capacity for joy.

Joy is the serious business of heaven.

C. S. Lewis

He will yet fill your mouth with laughter,
and your lips with shouts of joy.

JOB 8.21

Let the light of your face shine on us, O LORD.
You have put gladness in my heart
more than when their grain and wine abound.

PSALM 4.6-7

The prospect of the righteous is joy.

PROVERBS 10.28 NIV

For you shall go out in joy,
and be led back in peace;
the mountains and the hills before you
shall burst into song,
and all the trees of the field shall clap their hands.

ISAIAH 55.12

The Birth of the
Joy-Bringer

I n those days a decree went out
from Emperor Augustus that all the
world should be registered. This was
the first registration and was taken while
Quirinius was governor of Syria. All went to their
own towns to be registered. Joseph also went from
the town of Nazareth in Galilee to Judea, to the city of
David called Bethlehem, because he was descended
from the house and family of David. He went to be registered with Mary, to whom he was engaged and who was
expecting a child. While they were there, the time came for
her to deliver her child. And she gave birth to her firstborn
son and wrapped him in bands of cloth, and laid him in a
manager, because there was no place for them in the inn.

In that region there were shepherds living in the fields,
keeping watch over their flock by night. Then an angel of
the Lord stood before them, and the glory of the Lord shone

around them, and they were terrified. But the angel said to them, "Do not be afraid; for see—I am bringing you good news of great joy for all the people: to you is born this day in the city of David a Savior, who is the Messiah, the Lord. This will be a sign for you: you will find a child wrapped in bands of cloth and lying in a manger." And suddenly there was with the angel a multitude of the heavenly host, praising God and saying,

"Glory to God in the
highest heaven,
and on earth peace among those whom
he favors!"

When the angels had left them and gone into heaven, the shepherds said to one another, "Let us go now to Bethlehem and see this thing that has taken place, which the Lord has made known to us." So they went with haste and found Mary and Joseph, and the child lying in the manger. When they saw this, they made known what had been told them about this child; and all who heard it were amazed at what the shepherds told them. But Mary treasured all these words and pondered them in her heart. The shepherds returned, glorifying and praising God for all they had heard and seen, as it had been told them.

LUKE 2.1-20

Jesus came as the Joy-bringer. The joy we see in the happiest child is but a fraction of the joy that resides in the heart of God.

The gospel is a joyful message about Christ our Savior. Whoever preaches correctly preaches the gospel and nothing but joy. How can our hearts have a greater joy than knowing the Christ is given to us to be our own? The angel doesn't merely say "Christ was born," but also indicates that his birth is for us by saying, "your Savior."

So the nature of the gospel isn't just teaching the story and life of Christ but also personalizing it and offering it to all who believe. No matter how badly it's preached, my heart hears the gospel with joy. It penetrates all the way through and sounds wonderful.

MARTIN LUTHER

To miss out on joy is to miss

out on the reason for your

existence.

LEWIS SMEDES

The God of Joy

W e will not understand God until we understand this about him: "God is the happiest being in the universe." Joy is God's basic character. Joy is his eternal destiny. God is the happiest being in the universe.

And God's intent was that his creation would mirror his joy. The psalmist speaks of the sun, "which comes out like a bridegroom from his wedding canopy, and like a strong man runs its course with joy" (Psalm 19.5). This is not merely picturesque language; this is creation expressing God's own unwearying joy at simply being, at existing and knowing existence to be good. As products of God's creation, creatures made in his image, we are to reflect God's fierce joy in life.

This is why the Bible speaks not just about our need for joy in general, but a particular kind of joy that characterizes God.

After teaching on the need for obedience, Jesus told his friends that his aim was that they should be filled with joy, but not just *any* kind of joy: "I have said these things to you so that *my* joy may be in you, and that your joy may be complete" (John 15.11, emphasis mine).

The problem with people, according to Jesus, is not that we are too happy for God's taste, but that we are not happy enough.

JOY

is the echo of God's life within us.

JOSEPH MARMION

Rejoice in the Lord always;
again I will say,

REJOICE.

PHILIPPIANS 4.4

SATISFY *us in the morning with your* STEADFAST LOVE, *so that we may* rejoice *and be glad all our days.*

PSALM 90.14

Joy *is the most infallible sign of the presence of God.*

LEON BLOY

The Joy-Starved Man

Hank, as we'll call him, was a cranky guy. He did not smile easily and when he did, the smile often had a cruel edge to it, coming at someone else's expense. He had a knack for discovering islands of bad news in oceans of happiness. He would always find a cloud where others saw a silver lining.

Hank rarely affirmed anyone. He operated on the assumption that if you compliment someone, it might lead to a swelled head, so he worked to make sure everyone stayed humble. His was a ministry of cranial downsizing.

His native tongue was complaint. He carried judgment and disapproval the way a prisoner carries a ball and chain. Although he went to church his whole life, he was never unshackled.

A deacon in the church asked him one day, "Hank, are you happy?"

Hank paused to reflect, then replied without smiling, "Yeah."

"Well, tell your face," the deacon said. But so far as anybody knows, Hank's face never did find out about it.

Sometimes Hank's joylessness ended in comedy, but more often it produced sadness. His children did not know him. His son had a wonderful story about how he met his wife at a dance, but he never told his father because Hank did not approve of dancing.

Hank could not effectively love his wife or his children or people outside his family. He was easily irritated. He had little use for the poor, and a casual contempt for those whose accents or skin pigment differed from his own. Whatever capacity he once might have had for joy or wonder or gratitude atrophied. He critiqued and judged and complained, and his soul got a little smaller each year.

Hank was not changing. He was once a cranky young guy, and he grew up to be a cranky old man. But even more troubling than his lack of change was the fact that *nobody was surprised by it.* It was as if everyone simply expected that his soul would remain withered and sour year after year, decade after decade. No one seemed bothered by the condition. No church consultants were called in. No emergency meetings were held to probe the strange case of this person who followed the church's general guidelines for spiritual life and yet was nontransformed.

But the Bible puts joy in the non-optional category. Joy is a command. Joylessness is a serious sin, one that religious people are particularly prone to indulge in. It may be the sin most readily tolerated by the church. It is rarely the object of church discipline.

There is a being in this universe who wants you to live in sorrow, but it is *not* God.

Joy Is Strength

We are invited to rejoice in every moment of life because every moment of life is a gift. We don't earn it, can't control it, can't take a moment of it for granted. Every tick of the clock is a gift from God. Every day is a Dee Dah Day.

We have greatly underestimated the necessity of joy. Joy is strength. Its absence will create weakness. Or, in the words of Dallas Willard, "Failure to attain a deeply satisfying life always has the effect of making sinful actions seem good. Here lies the strength of temptation. . . . Normally, our success in overcoming temptation will be easier if we are basically happy in our lives. To cut off the joys and pleasures associated with our bodily lives and social existence as 'unspiritual,' then, can actually have the effect of *weakening* us in our efforts to do what is right."

Here is a key task for spiritual vitality:

We must arrange life

so that

sin no longer looks

good to us.

The time has come, strange as it sounds, for us to take joy seriously.

Joy appears now in little things. The big themes remain tragic. But a leaf fluttered in through a window this morning, as if supported by the rays of the sun, a bird settled on the fire escape, joy was in the taste of the coffee, joy accompanied me as I walked to the press. The secret of joy is the mastery of pain.

ANAIS LIN

This is the day that the LORD has made;
let us rejoice and be glad in it.

PSALM 118.24

Rejoice always, pray without ceasing, give thanks
in all circumstances; for this is the will of God
in Christ Jesus for you.

1 THESSALONIANS 5.16-18

But let the righteous be joyful;
let them exult before God;
let them be jubilant with joy.

PSALM 68.3

May the God of hope fill you with all joy and peace in
believing, so that you may abound in hope by the
power of the Holy Spirit.

ROMANS 15.13

The Joy Pursuit

Y ou can become a joyful person. With God's help, it really is possible. The biblical writers would not command it if it were not so. But joyfulness is a learned skill. You must take responsibility for your joy. Not your friend, not your parents, not your spouse, not your kids, not your boss can do it for you—your joy is your responsibility.

People who want to pursue joy especially need to practice the discipline of celebration. Celebration generally involves activities that bring pleasure—gathering with people we love, eating and drinking, singing and dancing. Spiritual celebration means doing them while reflecting on the wonderful God who has given us such wonderful gifts.

When we celebrate, we exercise our ability to see and feel goodness in the simplest gifts of God. We are able to take delight today in something we wouldn't have even noticed yesterday. Our capacity for joy increases.

The first step for pursuing joy is simply to begin now. *This* day, with all its shortcomings, is the great Dee Dah Day.

We all live with the illusion that joy will come someday when conditions change. We go to school and think we will be happy when we graduate. We are single and are convinced we will be happy when we get married. We get married and decide we will be happy someday when we have children. We have children and decide we will be happy when they grow up and leave the nest—then they do, and we think we were happier when they were still at home.

"This is God's day," the psalmist says. It is the day God made, a day that Christ's death has redeemed. If we are going to know joy, it must be in this day—today.

If we don't rejoice today, we will not rejoice at all. If we wait until conditions are perfect, we will still be waiting when we die. If we are going to rejoice, it must be in *this* day. This is the day that the Lord has made. This is the Dee Dah Day.

The surest mark of a Christian
is not faith, or even love, but joy.

SAMUEL M. SHOEMAKER

If you have no joy in your religion, there's a
leak in your Christianity somewhere.

BILLY SUNDAY

Joy is the gigantic secret of the Christian.

G. K. CHESTERTON

Make a joyful noise to the LORD, all the earth.

Worship the LORD with gladness;

come into his presence with singing.

Know that the LORD is God.

It is he that made us, and we are his;

we are his people, and the sheep of his pasture.

Enter his gates with thanksgiving,

and his courts with praise.

Give thanks to him, bless his name.

For the LORD is good;

his steadfast love endures forever,

and his faithfulness to all generations.

P SALM 100

Your Personal
Dee Dah Day

I f joy does not come easily for you, you may have to designate one day a week to be your personal Dee Dah Day, filled with pleasant things.

Devote a specific day to acts of celebration so that eventually joy will infuse your entire life. One day a week eat foods you love to eat, listen to music that moves your soul, play a sport that stretches and challenges you, read books that refresh your spirit, wear clothes that make you happy, surround yourself with beauty —and as you do these things, give thanks to God for his wonderful goodness. Reflect on what a gracious God he is to have thought of these gifts. Take the time to experience and savor joy, than direct your heart toward God so that you come to *know* he is the giver of "*every* good and perfect gift." Nothing is too small if it produces true joy in us and causes us to turn toward God in gratitude and delight.

If we are in *training* for a life characterized by joy, peace, and affection, we should assume that some of the practices are going to be downright enjoyable. Many of us need to discover "disciplines" such as celebration that will regularly produce in us rivers of wonder and gratitude.

God won't be offended by our happiness. In fact, he's offended by sadness and demands joy.

MARTIN LUTHER

A Surprise of Joy

E arly on the first day of the week, while it was still dark, Mary Magdalene came to the tomb and saw that the stone had been removed from the tomb. So she ran and went to Simon Peter and the other disciple, the one whom Jesus loved, and said to them, "They have taken the Lord out of the tomb, and we do not know where they have laid him."

Then Peter and the other disciple set out and went toward the tomb. The two were running together, but the other disciple outran Peter and reached the tomb first. He bent down to look in and saw the linen wrappings lying there, but he did not go in. Then Simon Peter came, following him, and went into the tomb. He saw the linen wrappings lying there, and the cloth that had been on Jesus' head, not lying with the linen wrappings but rolled up in a place by itself. Then the other disciple, who reached the tomb first, also went in, and he saw and believed; for as yet they did not understand the scripture, that he must rise from the dead. Then the disciples returned to their homes.

But Mary stood weeping outside the tomb. As she wept, she bent over to look into the tomb; and she saw two angels in white, sitting where the body of Jesus had been lying, one at the head and the other at the feet. They said to her, "Woman, why are you weeping?" She said to them, "They have taken away my Lord, and I do not know where they have laid him." When she had said this, she turned around and saw Jesus standing there, but she did not know that it was Jesus. Jesus said to her, "Woman, why are you weeping? Whom are you looking for?" Supposing him to be the gardener, she said to him, "Sir, if you have carried him away, tell me where you have laid him, and I will take him away." Jesus said to her, "Mary!" She turned and said to him in Hebrew, "Rabbouni!" (which means Teacher). Jesus said to her, "Do not hold on to me, because I have not yet ascended to the Father. But go to my brothers and say to them, 'I am ascending to my Father and your Father, to my God and your God.'" Mary Magdalene went and announced to the disciples, "I have seen the Lord"; and she told them that he had said these things to her.

When it was evening on that day, the first day of the week, and the doors of the house where the disciples had met were locked for fear of the Jews, Jesus came and stood among them and said, "Peace be with you!" After he said this, he showed them his hands and his side. Then the disciples rejoiced when they saw the Lord.

JOHN 20.1-20

MARKED BY JOY

We know that as Christians we are called to "come out and be separate," that our faith and spiritual commitment should make us different somehow. But if we are not marked by greater and greater amounts of love and joy, we will inevitably look for substitute ways of distinguishing ourselves from those who are not Christians. This deep pattern is almost inescapable for religious people: If we do not become changed from the inside-out, we will be tempted to find external methods to satisfy our need to feel that we're different from those outside the faith. If we cannot be transformed, we will settle for being informed or conformed.

Life counts—all of it. Every moment is potentially an opportunity to be guided by God into his way of living. Every moment is a chance to learn from Jesus how to live in the kingdom of God.

Jesus consistently focused on people's *center*: Are they oriented and moving toward the center of spiritual life (love of God and people), or are they moving away from it?

Overcoming Hurry Sickness

We suffer from what has come to be known as "hurry sickness." One of the great illusions of our day is that hurrying will buy us more time. But to be spiritually healthy you must ruthlessly eliminate hurry from your life.

Imagine for a moment that someone gave you this prescription, with the warning that your life depends on it. Hurry is the great enemy of spiritual life in our day. Hurry can destroy our souls. Hurry can keep us from living well.

Again and again, as we pursue spiritual life, we must do battle with hurry. For many of us the great danger is not that we will renounce our faith. It is that we will become so distracted and rushed and preoccupied that we will settle for a mediocre version of it. We will just skim our lives instead of actually living them.

We must ruthlessly eliminate hurry from our lives. This does not mean we will never be busy. Jesus often had much to do, but he never did it in a way that severed the life-giving connection between him and his Father. He never did it in a way that interfered with his ability to give love when love was called for. He observed a regular practice of withdrawing from activity for the sake of solitude and prayer. Jesus was often busy, but never hurried.

> Hurry is not just a disordered schedule. Hurry is a disordered heart.

It is because it kills love that hurry is the great enemy of spiritual life. Hurry lies behind much of the anger and frustration of modern life. Hurry prevents us from receiving love from the Father or giving it to his children. That's why Jesus never hurried. If we are to follow Jesus, we must ruthlessly eliminate hurry from our lives—because, by definition,

we can't

move faster than

the one we are following.

We can do this. We can become unhurried people. We can become patient people.

Jesus said to them, "Come away to a deserted place all by yourselves and rest a while."

MARK 6.31

Jesus said to his disciples: "Therefore I tell you, do not worry about your life, what you will eat, or about your body, what you will wear. Can any of you by worrying add a single hour to your span of life? If then you are not able to do so small a thing as that, why do you worry about the rest?"

Luke 12.22,25

So then, a sabbath rest still remains for the people of God; for those who enter God's rest also cease from their labors as God did from his.

Hebrews 4.9-10

For God alone my soul waits in silence; from him comes my salvation.

Psalm 62.1

The Cure for Hurrying

T he truth is, as much as we complain about it, we are drawn to hurry. It makes us feel important. It keeps the adrenaline pumping. It means we don't have to look too closely at our heart or our life. It keeps us from feeling our loneliness.

Solitude is the remedy for the busyness that charms. At its heart, solitude is primarily about *not* doing something. When we go into solitude, we withdraw from conversation, from the presence of others, from noise, from the constant barrage of stimulation. In solitude we get rid of all the stuff we use to convince ourselves that we are important or okay.

Solitude requires relentless perseverance. I find it helpful to think about solitude in two categories. We need brief periods of solitude on a regular basis—preferably each day, even at intervals during the day. But we also need, at great intervals, extended periods of solitude—half a day, a day, or a few days.

The press of busyness is like a charm. Its power swells . . . it reaches out seeking always to lay hold of ever-younger victims so that childhood or youth are scarcely allowed the quiet and the retirement in which the Eternal may unfold a divine growth.

Soren Kierkegaard

A solitude is the audience-chamber of God.

Walter Savage Landor

Solitude is the furnace of transformation.

Henri J. M. Nouwen

The Power of Prayer

U sually we think of events on earth being interrupted because of actions taken in heaven. However, in the eighth chapter of the book of Revelation, it is the other way around. All of heaven comes to a standstill. The endless songs and praises of heavenly hosts suddenly stop. Why? Because someone is praying. All of heaven stops so the prayers of the saints—your prayers and mine, every one of them—can rise before God. They are heard. They matter. Prayers of real human beings—like you and me—interrupt heaven.

Prayer changes things. It pays to haggle with God. You don't know how many people have been strengthened because you asked God to encourage them; how many people have been healed because you prayed for their bodies; how many spiritual runaways have come home because you prayed for their souls. None of us may ever know the true effects of our prayers this side of death. But we do know this: History belongs to the intercessors.

Prayer, perhaps more than any other activity, is the concrete expression of the fact that we are invited into a relationship with God. Prayer is "talking with God about what we are doing together," as Dallas Willard puts it. In addition to all the other work that gets done through prayer, perhaps the greatest work of all is the knitting of the human heart together with the heart of God. I have sat by the bedside of many people who have reached the end of their lives, and have heard them express regrets about many activities—years wasted in obsessions over work, time thrown away in pursuit of more money. I have never yet heard a person at the end of their life regret time they had spent in prayer. For where there is much prayer there is much love.

Prayer unites the soul to God.

JULIAN OF NORWICH

Nothing lies beyond the reach of prayer except that which lies outside the will of God.

ANONYMOUS

Ask, and it will be given you; search, and you will find; knock, and the door will be opened for you. For everyone who asks receives, and everyone who searches finds, and for everyone who knocks, the door will be opened.

MATTHEW 7.7-8

Hurry is the DEATH *of prayer.*

SAMUEL CHADWICK

The prayer of the righteous is powerful and effective.

JAMES 5.16

Prayer is a rising up and a drawing near to God in mind, and in heart, and in spirit.

ALEXANDER WHYTE

When you are praying, do not heap up empty phrases as the Gentiles do; for they think that they will be heard because of their many words. Do not be like them, for your Father knows what you need before you ask him.

MATTHEW 6.7-8

Jesus said, "So I tell you, whatever you ask for in prayer, believe that you have received it, and it will be yours."

MARK 11.24

Let the words of my mouth and the meditation of my heart be acceptable to you, O LORD, my rock and my redeemer.

PSALM 19.14

Prayer is the chief agency and activity whereby men align themselves with God's purpose. Prayer does not consist in battering the walls of heaven for personal benefits or the success of our plans. Rather, it is the committing of ourselves for the carrying out of His purposes. It is a telephone call to headquarters for orders. It is not bending God's will to ours, but our will to God's. In prayer, we tap vast reservoirs of spiritual power whereby God can find fuller entrance into the hearts of men.

G. Ashton Oldham

Listening for God's Guidance

I t is one thing to speak to God. It is another thing to listen. When we listen to God, we receive guidance from the Holy Spirit. Promptings may come as conviction of sin, an assurance of God's love, or a call to action. But they are crucial to the Spirit-guided life. We must learn to listen for the still, small voice.

Being open and receptive to the leadings of the Holy Spirit is a non-optional part of transformation. We can all learn how to be open to the promptings of the Spirit. They are not reserved for the elite or for leaders only or for "important people." They are not reserved for people who work as pastors or missionaries. They are not reserved for people who are "more spiritual" than you. The Holy Spirit can and will give direction to us if we desire it.

You may be right on the verge of experiencing this. Your adventure is about to begin.

In our day heaven and earth are on tiptoe waiting for the emerging of a Spirit-led, Spirit-intoxicated, Spirit-empowered people. All of creation watches expectantly for the springing up of a disciplined, freely gathered, martyr people who know in this life the life and power of the kingdom of God. It has happened before. It can happen again. . . .

Such a people will not emerge until there is among us a deeper, more profound experience of an Emmanuel of the Spirit—God with us, a knowledge that in the power of the Spirit Jesus has come to guide His people Himself, an experience of His leading that is as definite and as immediate as the cloud by day and fire by night.

RICHARD FOSTER

If I am to have a

relationship with God

that is in any sense

personal, I must be

open to the possibility

that sometimes God does

speak directly to me.

God Speaks to Moses

Moses was keeping the flock of his father-in-law Jethro, the priest of Midian; he led his flock beyond the wilderness, and came to Horeb, the mountain of God. There the angel of the LORD appeared to him in a flame of fire out of a bush; he looked, and the bush was blazing, yet it was not consumed. Then Moses said, "I must turn aside and look at this great sight; and see why the bush is not burned up." When the LORD saw that he had turned aside to see, God called to him out of the bush, "Moses, Moses!" And he said, "Here I am." Then he said, "Come no closer! Remove the sandals from your feet, for the place on which you are standing is holy ground." He said further, "I am the God of your father, the God of Abraham, the God of Isaac, and the God of Jacob." And Moses hid his face, for he was afraid to look at God.

Then the LORD said, "I have observed the misery of my people who are in Egypt; I have heard their cry on account of their taskmasters. Indeed, I know their sufferings, and I have come down to deliver them from the Egyptians, and to bring them up out of that land to a good and broad land, a land flowing with milk and honey, to the country of the Canaanites, the Hittites, the Amorites, the Perizzites, the Hivites, and the Jebusites. The cry of the Israelites has now come to me; I have also seen how the Egyptians oppress them. So come, I will send you to Pharaoh to bring my people, the Israelites, out of Egypt." But Moses said to God, "Who am I that I should go to Pharaoh, and bring the Israelites out of Egypt?" He said, "I will be with you; and this shall be the sign for you that it is I who sent you: when you have brought the people out of Egypt, you shall worship God on this mountain."

But Moses said to God, "If I come to the Israelites and say to them, 'The God of your ancestors has sent me to you,' and they ask me, 'What is his name?' what shall I say to them?" God said to Moses, "I AM WHO I AM." He said further, "Thus you shall say to the Israelites: 'I AM has sent me to you.'" God also said to Moses, "Thus you shall say to the Israelites, 'The Lᴏʀᴅ, the God of your ancestors, the God of Abraham, the God of Isaac, and the God of Jacob, has sent me to you.'

This is my name forever,
and this my title for all generations."

Exodus 3.1-15

God's purpose in

guidance is *not* to get us to

perform the right actions.

His purpose is to help us

become the right

kind of people.

There is a way of ordering our mental life on more than one level at once. On one level we may be thinking, discussing, seeing, calculating, meeting all the demands of external affairs. But deep within, behind the scenes, at a profounder level, we may also be in prayer and adoration, song and worship and a gentle receptiveness to divine breathings.

THOMAS KELLY

The Spirit's Voice in the Words of Others

G od speaks not only to us, but through us. Scripture is full of accounts of God's message being pronounced through human agency. God spoke to me one time, I believe, in most unusual circumstances through a friend named Lorraine.

Lorraine was well into her sixties when I met her. Her great passion was learning. Her house was mostly a place to store her books, just as her body was mostly a place to store her mind. As much as she loved learning, she loved teaching even more, and she taught Bible classes that attracted several hundred people.

This friend was one of the first people to insist to me that my true calling was to preach. "Now, honey," Lorraine would say, "you mustn't let someone talk you into doing something else. God made you to preach, and you won't be happy doing anything else."

It took a while, but I gradually decided Lorraine was right. I eventually moved away to become a full-time preacher, and we drifted out of touch.

Some years later, my family and I came back to visit the church. Lorraine was not attending; she had suffered a stroke and was confined to her bed. Her life was slowly slipping away.

Our visit to Lorraine's home was a bittersweet thing. She lay in a hospital bed in the front room. The mind that had been the source of pleasure to so many people no longer responded properly to the will of its owner. The books sat on the shelves, useless except as ornaments. Nancy and I both tried to talk with her.

We could see Lorraine trying to bring forth memories that had become inaccessible, but she couldn't. She wasn't quite able to place who this couple were. She spoke only in the language of vague murmurs and uncertain nods. After talking as best we could, we got up to leave.

Nancy was already out the door and I was on the threshold when I heard Lorraine's voice—only *this* time it was *her* voice. It sounded like the Lorraine we used to know.

"John Ortberg," she called. "Are you happy?"

"Yes," I said, too surprised to do anything but answer the question. "Yes, I really am."

"Good," she said. "Because God made you to preach. You should be full of joy when you do it, honey." And then Lorraine sank back into the pillow, exhausted, and she was gone again.

Lorraine did not know that we were facing a major decision at that time, and her comments about joy became enormously helpful. It became clear that one option would lead to a much greater sense of joy, even though in some ways it was the more difficult choice. God was, as best as I can discern it, speaking to us through a friend who could hardly speak at all.

. Much of the *a d v e n t u r e*

of Christian living involves

responsiveness to the guidance of

the Holy Spirit. This guidance

is not restricted to momentous

decisions. It is learned mainly as we

practice it on a continuing basis.

The LORD will guide you continually.

ISAIAH 58.11

Make me to know your ways, O LORD;
teach me your paths.
Lead me in your truth, and teach me,
for you are the God of my salvation;
for you I wait all day long.

PSALM 25.4-5

You are indeed my rock and my fortress,
for your name's sake lead me and guide me.
Into your hand I commit my spirit;
you have redeemed me, O LORD, faithful God.

PSALM 31.3,5

THE POWER FOR TRANSFORMATION

We cannot be transformed if we close ourselves off to the guiding power of the Holy Spirit. We must come to believe—mind-stretching as it sounds—that God really can and does personally attend to us. As long as we are going to pray to the God who spoke the creation into being, who communicated to prophets and priests and kings—and ordinary people—who wrote a thousand-page book we know as the Bible, and who refers to his Son as "the Word made flesh," then surely we accept the possibility that sometimes he may want to get in a word or two with us.

Speak, LORD, for your servant is listening.

1 SAMUEL 3.10

The Well-Ordered Heart

The secret of life is
pursuing one thing.

T here is a pursuit that is worthy of our devotion. There is a goal that is achievable even in the most desperate of situations. It will produce good far beyond our own little sphere of influence. It is something that our souls long for: the life we've always wanted.

It is the quest for what might be called a well-ordered heart. The balanced-life paradigm assumes that our problem is external—a disorder in our schedule or our job or our season of life. But the truly significant disorder is internal.

Augustine suggested that to have a well-ordered heart is to love the right thing, to the right degree, in the right way, with the right kind of love.

When the heart is well-ordered, we are not only increasingly free from sin, but also increasingly free from the *desire* to sin. If the heart were truly well-ordered, we would love people so much we would not *want* to deceive or manipulate or envy them. We would be transformed from the inside out.

Spiritual transformation cannot be orchestrated or controlled, but neither is it a random venture. We need a plan.

We need to develop what is called a "rule of life." A rule involves a rhythm for living in which we can grow more intimately connected to God. Consider how you might arrange your day around the pursuit of a well-ordered heart. Paul writes to the church at Colossae, as the climax of instruction on transformed living: "Whatever you do, in word or deed, do everything in the name of the Lord Jesus, giving thanks to God the Father through him" (Colossians 3.17).

Doing something in Jesus' name means to do it in his character. It means doing it as Jesus himself would do it if he were in your place. This flows right out of our understanding of discipleship. We sometimes miss the point of what Paul means because we tend to divide up life like a pie. But I believe Paul is quite serious about what he says. He is not simply using spiritual-sounding language. He really means it. We are invited to do *life* in Jesus' name.

It is unlikely that we will deepen our relationship with God in a casual or haphazard manner. There will be a need for some intentional commitment and some reorganization in our own lives. But there is nothing that will enrich our lives more than a deeper and clearer perception of God's presence in the routine of daily living.

<small>William Paulsell</small>

*Do not be conformed to this world, but be
transformed by the renewing of your minds,
so that you may discern what is the will of God—
what is good and acceptable and perfect.*

ROMANS 12.2

*You shall love the Lord your God with all your heart,
and with all your soul, and with all your mind.*

MATTHEW 22.37

*To set the mind on the flesh is death, but to set the
mind on the Spirit is life and peace.*

ROMANS 8.6

*Above all else, guard your heart,
for it is the wellspring of life.*

PROVERBS 4.23 NIV

Every moment is an opportunity to live in Jesus' name. All the everyday stuff of life can be filled with his presence—if you are.

Becoming a
Joyful Person

H ow is it possible to become a joyful
person in a pain-filled world? Look
at the promise that comes right near
the very end of the Bible:

Let us rejoice and exult
and give him the glory,
for the marriage of the Lamb has come,
and his bride has made herself ready.

REVELATION 19.17

Heaven's groom gets the bride.

The joy that is in store for God's people is so great that the
only image that can do it justice is the joy between a lover
and his beloved. Then we will see the wedding of which the
greatest weddings on this earth have only been a dim
foreshadowing.

Then God will dance with his people. Then joy will reign
undiminished and uninterrupted. Then will be fulfilled
the words of the prophet Isaiah, who was trying to
express the inexpressible:

You shall go out in joy,
and be led back in peace;
the mountains and the hills before you
shall burst into song,
and all the trees of the field shall clap their hands.

Isaiah 55.12

The apostle John tried to say this, too.

He will dwell with them;
they will be his peoples,
and God himself will be with them;
he will wipe every tear from their eyes.
Death will be no more;
mourning and crying and pain will be no more.

Revelation 21.3-4

Then will dawn the great Dee Dah Day that will never end.

The fruit of the Spirit is love, joy, peace, patience, kindness, generosity, faithfulness, gentleness, and self-control. There is no law against such things. And those who belong to Christ Jesus have crucified the flesh with its passions and desires. If we live by the Spirit, let us also be guided by the Spirit.

GALATIANS 5.22-25

If you have *faith*

the size of a mustard s e e d ,

you will say to this mountain, "MOVE

from here to there," and it *w i l l*

move; and N O T H I N G

will be impossible for Y O U .

MATTHEW 17.20–21

DOING

THE

Double-Dares

dare \dar\ *v.* to challenge someone to demonstrate courage

double-dare \dub' el dar\ *n.* an extreme challenge to demonstrate courage

faith \fath\ *n.* confidence or trust in God

The Daring Walk

A nd early in the morning Jesus came walking toward them on the sea. But when the disciples saw him walking on the sea, they were terrified, saying, "It is a ghost!" And they cried out in fear. But immediately Jesus spoke to them and said, "Take heart, it is I; do not be afraid."

Peter answered him, "Lord, if it is you, command me to come to you on the water." He said, "Come." So Peter got out of the boat, started walking on the water, and came toward Jesus. But when he noticed the strong wind, he became frightened, and beginning to sink, he cried out, "Lord, save me!" Jesus immediately reached out his hand and caught him, saying to him, "You of little faith, why did you doubt?"

When they got into the boat, the wind ceased. And those in the boat worshiped him, saying, "Truly you are the Son of God."

MATTHEW 14.25-32

God's Double Dare-ya

Peter's walk stands as an invitation to everyone who, like him, wants to step out in faith, who wants to experience something more of the power and presence of God. Let water-walking be a picture of doing with God's help what you could never do on your own. How does such a thing come about? There is a consistent pattern in Scripture of what happens in a life that God wants to use and improve:

There is always a call. God asks an ordinary person to engage in an act of extraordinary trust.

There is always fear. God has an inextinguishable habit of asking people to do things that are scary to them.

There is always reassurance. God promises his presence. God also promises to give whatever gifts are needed to fulfill his assignment.

There is always a decision. Sometimes people say yes to God's call. Sometimes they say no. But always people must decide.

There is always a changed life. Whatever the decision, yes or no, it always changes a life—and it changes the world that little life touches.

There is some aspect of your life in which God is calling you to walk with and to him, and when we say yes to his calling, it sets in motion a divine dynamic far beyond merely human power.

THE KEY TO ADVENTURE

I believe that God's general method for growing a deep, adventurous faith in us is by asking us to get out of our comfort zone. More than hearing a great talk, or reading a great book, God uses real-world challenges to develop our ability to trust in him.

We tend to seek a world of comfort. We try to construct manageable lives with some security and predictability to maintain the illusion that we are in control.

Then God walks by and shakes everything up. His call involves crisis, opportunity, often failure, generally fear, sometimes suffering, always the calling to a task too big for us. But there is no other way to grow faith and to partner with God.

It's not the critic who counts; not the man who points out how the strong man stumbles, or where the doer of deeds could have done better. The credit belongs to the man who is actually in the arena . . . who, at best, knows in the end the triumph of great achievement, and who, at the worst, if he fails, at least fails while daring greatly. So that his place will never be with those cold timid souls who know neither victory or defeat.

THEODORE ROOSEVELT

The Gift

ometime after Florence, my paternal grandmother, died, my grandfather called my mother with an unusual offer.

"Kathy," he said, in his heavy Swedish accent. "I was going through some of Florence's things in the attic when I came across a box of old dishes. I was going to get rid of them, but I noticed that they're blue—your favorite color. Why don't you take a look at them, and if you want them, they're yours; otherwise, I'll give them to the Salvation Army."

So my mother went through the attic, expecting to find some run-of-the-mill dinnerware. Instead, when she opened the box, she was looking at some of the most exquisite china she had ever seen. Each plate had been individually painted with a pattern of forget-me-nots. The cups were inlaid mother-of-pearl. The dishes and cups were rimmed with gold. The plates had been handcrafted in a Bavarian factory that was destroyed during the Second World War, so they were literally irreplaceable.

Yet my mother had been in the family for twenty years, and she had never seen this china before. She asked my father about it. He had grown up in the family—and he had never seen it, either.

Eventually they found out from some older family members the story of the china. When Florence was very young, she was given the china over a period of years. They were not a wealthy family, and the china was quite valuable, so she only got a piece at a time for gifts—confirmation, graduation, or a birthday.

Why had my parents never seen it? To know that, you have to know something about the character of Swedes. We are a cautious kind of people. We don't roll the dice easily. For instance, my two great aunts lived for eighty years in a beautiful Victorian home built by my great-grandfather in the 1800s. The most beautiful room in the house was a parlor. It was generally reserved for very special guests. No guest that special ever came to the house, so the parlor didn't get used much.

Whenever Florence received a piece of china—because it was so valuable, because if it was used it might get broken—she would wrap it very carefully in tissue, put it in a box, and store it in the attic for a very special occasion. No occasion that special ever came along. So my grandmother went to her grave with the greatest gift of her life unopened and unused.

Then my mother was given the dishes. She uses them promiscuously—every chance she has. They have finally made it out of the box.

I believe there is something—Someone—inside

us who tells us there is more to life than sitting

in your comfort zone. You were made for some-

thing more than merely avoiding failure. There

is something inside you that wants to walk on

the water—to leave the comfort of routine exis-

tence and abandon yourself to the high adven-

ture of following God.

Using Gifts

Any time a gift is given, the recipient must choose to respond in one of two ways. The first way says, *This gift is so valuable it can't be risked.* Those who follow the first way realize that when the gift is brought out of the box and into the open, things may not always go well. The gift may be poorly used sometimes. It may not always be admired by others the way we want. It may even get broken. Taking the gift out of the box is always a risk.

The second way says, *This gift is so valuable it must be risked.* Those who follow the second way understand that if the gift is not brought out of the box, it will never be used at all. To leave the gift in the box is to thwart the desire of the giver. *There is no tragedy like the tragedy of the unopened gift.*

You, too, have been given a gift. Along with the gift, you have been given a choice—whether or not you will open and use what was given to you. Is your life following the first way or the second?

Everybody receives a gift. We are all called by God. We are all equipped and expected to contribute. Every gift is chosen by the master. I may like my gift, or I may not. I may torture myself by desiring what belongs to another, but it will do me no good. No one decides on his or her giftedness.

God has been very generous. There are no no-talent people in his world. Not only that, God himself offers to partner with you in your life. He offers to guide you when you need wisdom, encourage you when you falter, pick you up when you sink, and forgive you when you stray. He offers us himself as the best gift of all.

Faith is using one's endowed giftedness

to serve the world with excellence and,

through that service, to love and honor

God! The calling that fully engages what

God has given you is a holy task!

ARTHUR MILLER

*Each [person] has a particular gift from God, one
having one kind and another a different kind.*

1 CORINTHIANS 7.7

*Let your light shine before others, so that they
may see your good works and give glory to
your Father in heaven.*

MATTHEW 5.16

*Every generous act of giving, with every perfect gift,
is from above, coming down from the Father
of lights, with whom there is no variation
or shadow due to change.*

JAMES 1.17

For the gifts and the calling of God are irrevocable.

ROMANS 11.29

Because you were made in God's image, you were also created to do work. You were made to create, lead, study, organize, heal, cultivate, or teach. You have a purpose—a design that is central to God's dream for the human race. We are, first of all, according to Scripture, called to know God, to receive his love and mercy, and to be his children. We are called to live in the reality of his kingdom and to have Christ formed in us.

As a crucial part of your calling, you were given certain gifts, talents, longings, and desires. To identify these with clarity, to develop them with skill, and to use them joyfully and humbly to serve God and his creation is central to why you were created.

What we do matters immensely. It is worth devoting our best energy to. *We are on a mission from God.*

We didn't give ourselves the personalities, talents, or longings we were born with. When we fulfill these—these gifts from beyond ourselves—it is like fulfilling something we were meant to do . . . the creator of all things knows the name of each of us—knows thoroughly, better than we do ourselves, what is in us, for he put it there and intends for us to do something with it—something that meshes with his intentions for many other people. . . . Even if we do not always think of it that way, each of us was given a calling—by fate, by chance, by destiny, by God. Those who are lucky have found it.

MICHAEL NOVAK

Follow Your Calling

A calling is something you discover, not something you choose. You also have a nature with your own potential and limits. Frederich Buechner wrote that calling is "the place where your deep gladness meets the world's deep need." It is not hard to figure out where the world's deep need is. It is everywhere! What turns out to be more difficult then you might expect is discovering where your deep gladness lies. What work brings you joy? For what do you have desire and passion—for these, too, are gifts from God. This is why giftedness is about more than just talents—it includes passion.

God doesn't call us in a way that violates our "raw material." Where God calls, God gifts. Natural talent alone is not enough to honor a calling from God. I will need ideas, strength, and creativity beyond my own resources to do what God asks of me. It will have to be God and me doing it together. We are not called just to work *for* God. We are called to work *with* God.

Lead a life worthy of the calling

to which you have been called, with all humility

and gentleness, with patience, bearing with one

another in love, making every effort to maintain the

unity of the Spirit in the bond of peace

EPHESIANS 4.1–3

Some people say, "God will never ask me to do something I can't do." I have come to the place in my life that, if the assignment I sense God is giving me is something that I know I can handle, I know it is probably not from God. The kind of assignments God gives in the Bible are always God-sized. They are always beyond what people can do, because he wants to demonstrate his nature, his strength, his provision, and his kindness to his people and to a watching world. This is the only way the world will come to know him.

Don't Look Down

The first time I ever skied was in the Swiss Alps. A friend who ran a winter sports camp flew my wife and me from Scotland, where we were living on the meager funds of a graduate fellowship, paid for our ski rentals, and bought us lift tickets. After two trips down the bunny slope, I told my wife, an avid skier, that I was ready for something more adventurous. We got on a chair lift, and it quickly rose hundreds of feet off the ground. My wife does not like heights. She grabbed the metal pole that stood between us and wrapped herself around it like a boa constrictor.

"Honey," she said, paraphrasing Ken Davis. "I love you. You're my husband, and I'd do anything for you. But do you see this post? This is *my* post. If you touch this post, you'll meet Jesus today."

"Don't look down," I suggested.

We got off the chair lift and took something called a T-bar up the final ascent. Unfortunately, when we were almost to the top of the mountain, we fell off the T-bar. For a while we lay in the snow, waiting for the St. Bernard who never came. Dozens of skiers whizzed up the Alp beside us, yelling advice to us in German.

Another couple fell off (or jumped out of pity) at the same point. Hans could speak a little English, and he guided us for an hour through hip-deep snow to the nearest slope. The slope was marked by a black diamond with skull and crossbones. It went downhill at an angle of about eighty-five degrees.

Hans then gave me the only skiing lesson I have ever had. "Don't look down," he said. "You will be frightened by the slope and overwhelmed by the distance. When new skiers look down, they panic; and when they face straight ahead on a slope this steep—" He made a whistling sound and a motion with his hand that was not encouraging. "I think you can make it." (The word *think* bothered me a little.) "Just remember one thing: Don't look down."

"Don't look down" became the number one rule of the day. I would not look down for anything. Six-year-old skiers would ski between my legs to try to tempt me to watch them go down. I set a record for Most Zigzag Turns that day. People would ski past me, take the chair lift up, go past me again—just to see how many times they could lap me.

I suspect I pulled off the ugliest ski run that particular Alp had ever seen. Even when making snowplow turns, I would arrange whenever possible to execute them in front of small children so they could break my fall if necessary.

I got only one thing right: I never looked down. I became the world's expert at not looking down. It wasn't pretty, but it got me to the bottom of the hill.

There is a condition of the mind that is essential for us to live the kind of lives we are longing for. Call it hope, trust, or confidence. It is the single greatest difference between those who try and those who give up. When it is lost we are sunk. Don't look down.

I will hope continually,
and will praise you yet more and more.

PSALM 71.14

Now hope that is seen is not hope. For who hopes for
what is seen? But if we hope for what we do not see,
we wait for it with patience.

ROMANS 8.24-25

Truly the eye of the LORD is on those who fear him,
on those who hope in his steadfast love.

PSALM 33.18

Hope deferred makes the heart sick,
but a desire fulfilled is a tree of life.

PROVERBS 13.12

Hope Defined

Hope is the fuel that the human heart runs on. A car crash or a diving accident can paralyze a body, but the death of hope paralyzes the spirit.

Hope is what prompts a young man and woman to stand before a preacher and promise, "I do," even though they have no guarantees.

Hope is what fuels the same couple, many years later, after broken promises and broken hearts, to give their promise another try.

Hope is why human beings keep bringing children into a fallen world.

Hope is why there are hospitals and universities.

Hope is why there are therapists and consultants and why the Cubs keep going to spring training.

Pablo Casals continued to practice the cello five hours a day even though he was recognized as the world's greatest cellist, even when he had grown ancient enough that the effort exhausted him. Someone asked him what made him do it. "I think I'm getting better," he replied.

THAT is

Hope.

The word which God has written on the brow of every man is Hope.

VICTOR HUGO

Hope is the parent of faith.

CYRUS AUGUSTUS BARTOL

Hope arouses, as nothing else can arouse, a passion for the possible.

WILLIAM SLOANE COFFIN

The Hope-Filled Mind

I read recently about a woman who had been diagnosed with cancer and was given three months to live. Her doctor told her to make preparations to die, so she contacted her pastor and told him how she wanted things arranged for her funeral service—which songs she wanted to have sung, what Scriptures should be read, what words should be spoken—and that she wanted to be buried with her favorite Bible.

But before he left, she called out to him, "One more thing."

"What?"

"This is important. I want to be buried with a fork in my right hand." The pastor did not know what to say. No one had ever made such a request before. So she explained. "In all my years going to church functions, whenever food was involved, my favorite part was when whoever was cleaning dishes of the main course would lean over and say, *You can keep your fork.*

"It was my favorite part because I knew that it meant something great was coming. It wasn't Jell-O. It was something with substance—cake or pie—biblical food.

"So I just want people to see me there in my casket with a fork in my hand, and I want them to wonder, *What's with the fork?* Then I want you to tell them. *Something better is coming. Keep your fork.*"

The pastor hugged the woman good-bye. And soon after, she died.

At the funeral service, people saw the dress she had chosen, saw the Bible she loved, and heard the songs she loved, but they all asked the same question: "What's with the fork?"

The pastor explained that this woman, their friend, wanted them to know that for her—or for anyone who dies in Christ—this is not a day of defeat. It is a day of celebration. The real party is just starting.

Something better is coming.

Think on These Things

W e can survive the loss of an extraordinary number of things, but no one can outlive hope. When it is gone, we are done. Therefore the capacity to stay focused on the presence and power of God in our lives becomes supremely important. When we forget this simple truth, we are like a steelworker walking on an I-beam three hundred feet in the air who begins looking down. When we become more focused on the overwhelming nature of the storm than the overwhelming presence of God, we are in trouble.

For one who believes in God, the hinge point is not simply what *I'm* capable of. The real question is what might God want to do through me. "I can do everything through Christ who gives me strength" (Philippians 4.13 NIV). Now, this is not a blank check. In writing these words, the apostle Paul did not intend for us to understand that being a Christian means I can hit more home runs than Mark McGwire and hit higher notes than Pavarotti. It means I have great confidence that I can face whatever life throws at me, that I never need to give up, that my efforts have potency—because of the One at work within me.

Our ability to live in hope—to remain focused on Christ during the storm—is largely dependent on what we feed our minds.

The way you think creates your attitudes; the way you think shapes your emotions; the way you think governs your behavior; the way you think deeply influences your immune system and vulnerability to illness. Everything about you flows out of the way you think.

Isaiah says, "Thou wilt keep him in perfect peace, whose mind is stayed on thee" (Isaiah 26.3 KJV). It all depends on where your mind stays. If you really want to become a certain kind of person—a hopeful person focused on Christ—you must begin to think thoughts that will produce those characteristics. So we understand why Paul said, "Whatever is true, whatever is honorable, whatever is just, whatever is pure, whatever is pleasing, whatever is commendable, if there is any excellence and if there is anything worthy of praise, think about these things" (Philippians 4.8). When we focus on Christ, these are the kinds of thoughts he will inspire you to think. Therefore you must put your mind in a place that will lead you to think hope-producing thoughts. You need to expose your mind to those resources, books, tapes, people, and conversations that will incline you toward confidence in God.

Research has shown that one's thought life influences every aspect of one's being.

ARCHIBALD HART

To think well is to serve God in the interior court.

THOMAS TRAHERNE

Occupy your minds with good thoughts, or the enemy will fill them with bad ones: unoccupied they cannot be.

SIR THOMAS MORE

I arise today through God's strength to pilot me:
God's might to uphold me,
God's wisdom to guide me,
God's eye to look before me,
God's ear to hear me,
God's word to speak for me,
God's hand to guard me.
Christ with me, Christ before me,
Christ behind me,
Christ in me, Christ beneath me, Christ above me,
Christ on my right, Christ on my left,
Christ when I lie down, Christ when I sit down,
Christ when I arise.
Christ in the heart of every one who thinks of me,
Christ in the mouth of every one who speaks of me,
Christ in every eye that sees me,
Christ in every ear that hears me.
I arise today
through a mighty strength,
the invocation of the Trinity.

SAINT PATRICK

Now the LORD said to Abram, "Go from your country and your kindred and your father's house to the land that I will show you. I will make of you a great nation, and I will bless you, and make your name great, so that you will be a blessing."

So Abram went, as the LORD had told him; and Lot went with him. Abram was seventy-five years old when he departed from Haran.

The LORD appeared to Abraham by the oaks of Mamre, as he sat at the entrance of his tent in the heat of the day. He looked up and saw three men standing near him. When he saw them, he ran from the tent entrance to meet them, and bowed down to the ground. He said, "My lord, if I find favor with you, do not pass by your servant. Let a little water be brought, and wash your feet, and rest yourselves under the tree. Let me bring a little bread, that you may refresh yourselves, and after that you may pass on—since you have come to your servant." So they said, "Do as you have said." And Abraham hastened into the tent to Sarah, and said, "Make ready quickly three measures of choice flour, knead it, and make cakes." Abraham ran to the herd, and took a calf, tender and good, and gave it to the servant, who hastened to prepare it. Then he took curds and milk and the calf that he had prepared, and set it before them; and he stood by them under the tree while they ate.

They said to him, "Where is your wife Sarah?" And he said, "There, in the tent." Then one said, "I will surely return to you in due season, and your wife Sarah shall have a son." And Sarah was listening at the tent entrance behind him. Now Abraham and Sarah were old, advanced in age; it had ceased to be with Sarah after the manner of women. So Sarah laughed to herself, saying, "After I have grown old, and my husband is old, shall I have pleasure?" The LORD said to Abraham, "Why did Sarah laugh, and say, 'Shall I indeed bear a child, now that I am old?' Is anything too wonderful for the LORD? At the set time I will return to you, in due season, and Sarah shall have a son."

The LORD dealt with Sarah as he had said, and the LORD did for Sarah as he had promised. Sarah conceived and bore Abraham a son in his old age, at the time of which God had spoken to him. Abraham gave the name Isaac to his son whom Sarah bore him.

And Abraham circumcised his son Isaac when he was eight days old, as God had commanded him. Abraham was a hundred years old when his son Isaac was born to him. Now Sarah said, "God has brought laughter for me; everyone who hears will laugh with me." And she said, "Who would ever have said to Abraham that Sarah would nurse children? Yet I have borne him a son in his old age."

GENESIS 12.1-2,4; 18.1-14; 21.1-7

God comes to Abraham when he is seventy-five and tells him he is going to be a father, the ancestor of a great nation. How long was it before that promise was fulfilled? Twenty-five years. Abraham had to wait.

God told the Israelites that they would leave their slavery in Egypt and become a nation. But the people had to wait four hundred years.

God told Moses he would lead the people to the Promised Land. But they had to wait forty years in the wilderness.

Waiting may be the single hardest thing we are called to do. So it is frustrating when we turn to the Bible and find that God himself, who is all-powerful and all-wise, keeps saying to his people, "Wait."

Waiting is so closely associated with faith that sometimes the two words are used interchangeably.

Be still before the LORD, and wait patiently for him.

PSALM 37.7

Wait for the LORD, and keep to his way,
and he will exalt you to inherit the land.

PSALM 37.34

Wait for the LORD;
be strong, and let your heart take courage;
wait for the LORD!

PSALM 27.14

It is good that one should wait quietly
for the salvation of the LORD.

LAMENTATIONS 3.26

Waiting is our destiny as

creatures who cannot by themselves

bring about what they hope for.

We wait in the darkness for

a flame we cannot light,

we wait in fear for a happy ending

we cannot write.

We wait for a not yet

that feels like a not ever.

Waiting is the hardest work of hope.

LEWIS SMEDES

⊙ ⊘ ⊙ ⊘ ⊙ ⊙ ⊘ ⊙ ⊙ ⊙ ⊘ ⊙ ⊙

Waiting is not just something we have to do while we get what we want. It is part of the process of becoming what God wants us to be.

—〜〜—

God's work in us while we wait is as important as what it is we think we are waiting for. Waiting means that we give God the benefit of the doubt that he knows what he is doing.

—〜〜—

Because waiting reminds us that we are waiting for someone, the single most important activity in waiting is prayer. Prayer allows us to wait without worry.

Even youths will faint and be weary,
and the young will fall exhausted;
but those who wait for the LORD
shall renew their strength,
they shall mount up with wings like eagles,
they shall run and not be weary,
they shall walk and not faint.

ISAIAH 40.30-31

Soaring, Running, Walking

I f you are waiting on God these days, you need to know that this passage in Isaiah holds a wonderful promise attached to this waiting. We must live these words—soaring, running, and walking—"one line at a time."

Sometimes you will mount up and soar on wings of eagles. This is a beautiful picture. Ornithologists say birds have three methods of flight. The first is flapping—keeping their wings in constant motion to counteract gravity. Hummingbirds can flap up to seventy times per second. Flapping keeps you up in the air, but it is a lot of work. Flapping is an awkward, clumsy business. I spend a lot of time flapping around. It gets me from here to there, but there is not a lot of grace involved.

A second flight method is gliding. Here the bird builds up enough speed, then coasts downward a while. It is much more graceful than flapping, but unfortunately it does not get the bird very far. Reality in the form of gravity sets in quickly. Gliding is nice, but it does not last.

Then there is the third way—soaring. Only a few birds, like eagles, are capable of this. Eagles' wings are so strong that they are capable of catching rising currents of warm air—thermal winds that go straight up from the earth—and without moving a feather can soar up to great heights. Eagles have been clocked at up to 80 mph without flapping at all. They just soar on invisible columns of rising air.

Isaiah says that for those who wait on the Lord, times will come when they soar. You catch a gust of the spirit. Sometimes in your life you will be in an era of spiritual soaring. Maybe you are there right now. You find yourself simply borne up by God's power. You are soaring with the Spirit.

Sometimes we are not soaring, but we are able to run and not grow weary. If this is where you are, your life isn't feeling effortless. You have to do some flapping. But with persistence and determination you know you are running the race. Your time will come. Just keep running.

Sometimes we will not be soaring, and we cannot run. In those times all we can do is walk and not faint. All we can do is say, "God, I'll hang on. I won't let go. I will obey you. I'll just keep walking."

We have some very fast runners in our world. We have some eagles that soar much higher than we can see. It is a hard thing to be a walker when you are surrounded by racers and eagles. But sometimes walking is the best we can offer God. He understands all about that. Walking counts, too.

Keep walking. What we wait for is not more important then what happens to us while we are waiting. It is just a matter of time.

Having faith

does not mean

never having doubts

or questions.

It does mean

remaining

obedient.

Living with a Soooo Big God

I strongly believe that the way we live is a consequence of the size of our God. The problem many of us have is that our God is too small. We are not convinced that we are absolutely safe in the hands of a fully competent, all-knowing, ever-present God.

When we wake up in the morning, what happens if we live with a small God?

We live in a constant state of fear and anxiety because everything depends on *us*. Our mood will be governed by our circumstances. We will live in a universe that leaves us deeply vulnerable. If we don't live in the security of a big God's acceptance, we become slaves to what others think of us. We may try to get credit for something at work that does not belong to us because we don't trust in a Big God who sees in secret and will one day give reward.

If somebody gets mad at us or disapproves, we will get all twisted up in knots—we will not have the security of knowing that a giant God is watching out for us.

When human beings shrink God, they offer prayer without faith, work without passion, service without joy, suffering without hope. It results in fear, retreat, loss of visions, and failure to persevere.

As soon as children are old enough to speak, one of the first questions parents ask is, "How big are you?" Children always give the same answer, "I'm *soooo* big!"

We teach our children to say this because we know that the way they think of themselves matters. We don't want them to think of themselves as small, weak, and lacking adequate strength to handle the challenges of life.

But now I have a more important question: How big is your *God?*

Lord, help me to do great things as though they were little, since I do them with your power; and little things as though they were great, since I do them in your name.

BLAISE PASCAL

David and His
Soooo Big God

King Saul and the Israelites gathered and encamped in the valley of Elah, and formed ranks against the Philistines. And there came out from the camp of the Philistines a champion named Goliath, of Gath, whose height was six cubits and a span. He had a helmet of bronze on his head, and he was armed with a coat of mail; the weight of the coat was five thousand shekels of bronze. He had greaves of bronze on his legs and a javelin of bronze slung between his shoulders. The shaft of his spear was like a weaver's beam, and his spear's head weighed six hundred shekels of iron; and his shield-bearer went before him. And the Philistine said, "Today I defy the ranks of Israel! Give me a man, that we may fight together." When Saul and all Israel heard these words of the Philistine, they were dismayed and greatly afraid.

Now David was the son of Jesse, who had eight sons. David was the youngest; the three eldest followed Saul, but David went back and forth from Saul to feed his father's sheep at Bethlehem. For forty days the Philistine came forward and took his stand, morning and evening.

Jesse said to his son David, "Take for your brothers an ephah of this parched grain and these ten loaves, and carry them quickly to the camp to your brothers." David rose early in the morning, left the sheep with a keeper, took the provisions, and went as Jesse had commanded him. As he talked with his brothers, the champion, the Philistine of Gath, Goliath by name, came up out of the ranks of the Philistines, and spoke the same words as before. And David heard him.

David said to Saul, "Let no one's heart fail because of him; your servant will go and fight with this Philistine. The LORD, who saved me from the paw of the lion and from the paw of the bear, will save me from the hand of this Philistine." So Saul said to David, "Go, and may the LORD be with you!"

David took his staff in his hand, and chose five smooth stones from the wadi, and put them in his shepherd's bag, in the pouch; his sling was in his hand, and he drew near to the Philistine.

When the Philistine looked and saw David, he disdained him, for he was only a youth, ruddy and handsome in appearance. And the Philistine cursed David by his gods. But David said to the Philistine, "You come to me with sword and spear and javelin; but I come to you in the name of the LORD of hosts, the God of the armies of Israel, whom you have defied. This very day the LORD will deliver you into my hand, and I will strike you down and cut off your head; so that all the earth may know that there is a God in Israel, and that all this assembly may know that the LORD does not save by sword and spear; for the battle is the LORD's and he will give you into our hand."

When the Philistine drew nearer to meet David, David ran quickly toward the battle line to meet the Philistine. David put his hand in his bag, took out a stone, slung it, and struck the Philistine on his forehead; the stone sank into his forehead, and he fell face down on the ground.

So David prevailed over the Philistine with a sling and a stone, striking down the Philistine and killing him; there was no sword in David's hand.

FROM 1 SAMUEL 17

Living a Life of Worship

H ow can I come to believe in the sufficiency of Christ for my life the way I now believe in gratitude? How can I live in a way that reflects the fact that I follow a God who is *sooo big?*

There is a word for the process by which human beings come to perceive and declare the vastness, worthiness, and strength of God. It is called worship.

Worship is not about filling God's unmet ego needs. God has made us so that when we experience something transcendentally great, we have a need to praise it. Our experience is incomplete until we can wrap words around it. When we see the Grand Tetons for the first time, a double rainbow, or a nest of baby herons getting ready for their first flight, something in our spirits demands that we express the joy we receive.

We are to worship God, not because his ego needs it, but because without worship, our experience and enjoyments of God are not complete. We worship God not so much because he needs it, but because *we* do.

When we reflect

on what *God* has done

and *respond* in worship,

our understanding

of God *grows*.

For nothing will be impossible with God.

LUKE 1.37

Now to him who by the power at work within us is able to accomplish abundantly far more than all we can ask or imagine, to him be glory in the church and in Christ Jesus to all generations, forever and ever. Amen.

EPHESIANS 3.20–21

What is impossible for mortals is possible for God.

LUKE 18.27

The LORD your God, who is present with you, is a great and awesome God.

DEUTERONOMY 7.21

If the Lord be with us, we have no cause of fear. His eye is upon us, His arm over us, His ear open to our prayer—His grace sufficient, His promise unchangeable.

John Newton

A Time for Growing

A friend and I were going to spend two weeks preaching in Ethiopia when it was still under Marxist rule. The underground churches that invited me over asked if we would bring fifty study Bibles with us. I had reservations about smuggling Bibles. But we decided to give it a shot. The churches we served donated the Bibles needed; in fact, just before we left, one woman came up and pressed an extra one in my hands, so we actually took fifty-one.

Sure enough, the customs agent opened one of the suitcases and confiscated the Bibles. A few days later we received a call that the head customs official wanted an interview with the leaders of the churches. We feared the worst—church leaders in Ethiopia spent so much time in prison they referred to it as "the university." (This is where God would send his leaders when he really wanted them to grow. Like the biblical Joseph, some of them would actually be put in charge by the guards when the guards wanted to go on break. They would take the bullets out of their rifles and hand them to the Christian prisoners to stand watch till they got back!) At best we were hoping we might be able to get the Bibles out of their hands through a bribe.

Imagine our surprise when the official said, "These Bibles are illegal. You may take them out on one condition—you must tell no one. I want to keep one for myself."

My God got a little larger that day. Soooo big!

Every time someone steps out in faith, their God gets a little bigger.

When human beings step out in faith, they are never quite the same. Their worship is never quite the same. Their world is never quite the same. Whatever the results, whether they sink or swim, something will have changed.

This is true for you. From this point on, for the rest of your life, each time you trust God and seek to discern and obey his calling on your life, your God will get bigger, and your worship will grow deeper, richer, and stronger.

That is because Jesus is not finished yet. He is still looking for people who will dare to trust him. He is still looking for people who will refuse to allow fear to have the final word. He is still looking for people who refuse to be deterred by failure. He is still passing by. And this is your one and only opportunity to answer his call.

This is

your CHANCE

of a lifetime.

*The only thing that counts is
faith working through love.*

GALATIANS 5.6

*I have fought the good fight,
I have finished the race, I have kept the faith.*

2 TIMOTHY 4.7

*Fight the good fight of the faith;
take hold of the eternal life, to which
you were called and for which you made the
good confession in the presence of many witnesses.*

1 TIMOTHY 6.12

*Trust in the LORD forever,
for in the LORD GOD
you have an everlasting rock.*

ISAIAH 26.4

Knowing when to take a risk

does not only demand courage;

it also demands the wisdom to ask

the right questions, the discernment to

recognize the voice of the Master, and

the patience to wait for his command.

SOURCES

Luther, Martin. *By Faith Alone.* Copyright 1998 by Jim Galvin. Grand Rapids, MI: World Publishing, 1998.

Ortberg, John. *If You Want to Walk on Water, You've Got to Get Out of the Boat.* Copyright 2001 by John Ortberg. Grand Rapids, MI: Zondervan, 2001.

Ortberg, John. *The Life You've Always Wanted.* Copyright 1997, 2002 by John Ortberg. Grand Rapids, MI: Zondervan, 2002.

Ortberg, John. *Love Beyond Reason.* Copyright 1998 by John Ortberg. Grand Rapids, MI: ZondervanPublishingHouse, 1998.

At Inspirio we love to hear from you—your stories, your feedback, and your product ideas. Please send your comments to us by way of e-mail at icares@zondervan.com.